# Mini Artist
# Papercraft

Toby Reynolds

WINDMILL
BOOKS
New York

Published in 2015 by Windmill Books, An Imprint of Rosen Publishing
29 East 21st Street, New York, NY 10010

Editor for Windmill: Joshua Shadowens

Photo Credits: Illustrations by Fiona Gowen; Images on pages 2 and 3 © fotolia.com.

Library of Congress Cataloging-in-Publication Data

Reynolds, Toby, author.
 Papercraft / by Toby Reynolds.
     pages cm. — (Mini artist)
 Includes index.
 ISBN 978-1-4777-9123-3 (library binding) — ISBN 978-1-4777-9124-0 (pbk.) —
 ISBN 978-1-4777-9125-7 (6-pack)
 1. Paper work—Juvenile literature. 2. Handicraft—Juvenile literature. I. Title.
 TT870.R4625 2015
 745.54—dc23
                                   2014001202


Manufactured in the United States of America

CPSIA Compliance Information: Batch #WS14WM: For Further Information contact Windmill Books, New York, New York at 1-866-478-0556

Mini Artist **Papercraft**

# Contents

# Getting Started

The projects in this book use lots of art **materials** that you will already have at home. Any missing materials can be found in an art supply store.

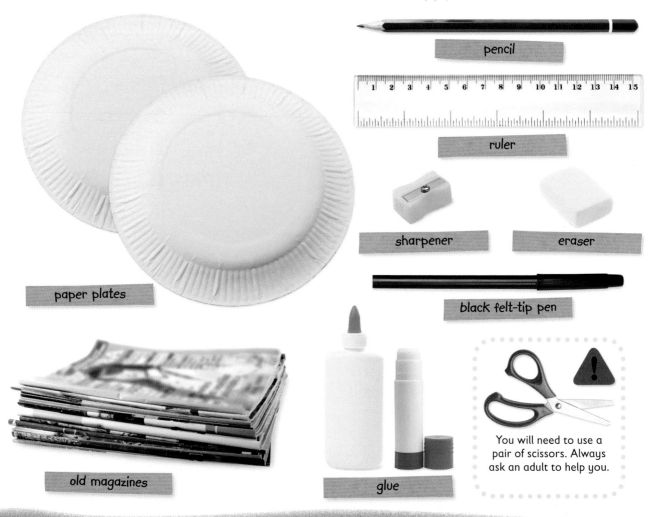

pencil

ruler

sharpener

eraser

black felt-tip pen

paper plates

old magazines

glue

You will need to use a pair of scissors. Always ask an adult to help you.

aluminum foil

books

# Handy Hint

Wrapping paper, newspaper or pieces of old wallpaper are excellent for papercraft projects. Why not start a collection?

Here is a selection of the paper you will need to complete all the papercraft projects.

# House on a Hill

This pretty house is a fun project to make. You'll need colored paper, glue and a pair of scissors.

**1** Start with a piece of blue paper for the background. Cut a green strip of paper into the shape of bushes.

**2** Add some pale green paper under the bushes. The pale green paper will be the grass in your picture.

**3** Cut a yellow square for the house and a red triangle for the roof. Now glue all of the pieces down.

**4** Cut two rectangles out of red paper. Glue one to the roof for a chimney and use the other to make the door.

**5** Cut two small squares from some blue paper and glue these onto the front of the house for windows.

**6** Add some trees, flowers, grass and clouds in the sky to finish your picture.

# Fancy Fish

To make this exciting underwater picture you will need colored paper, glue and a pair of scissors.

**1** Start with some blue paper for the background. Glue some brown paper along the bottom for the sea floor.

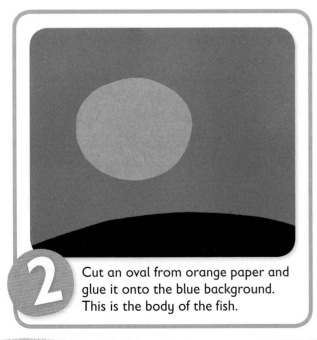

**2** Cut an oval from orange paper and glue it onto the blue background. This is the body of the fish.

**3** Cut some more shapes from the orange paper for the tail and fins. Glue these onto the body.

**4** Now use a circle of white paper and a smaller circle of black paper to make the eye. Glue them into position.

**5** Cut long strips of green paper for plants in the water. You can add red paper stripes to the body.

**6** Finish your picture by adding more fish and gluing blue circles on top for bubbles.

# Time for a Party

You can make these fun cards using card stock, colored paper, felt-tip pens and scissors.

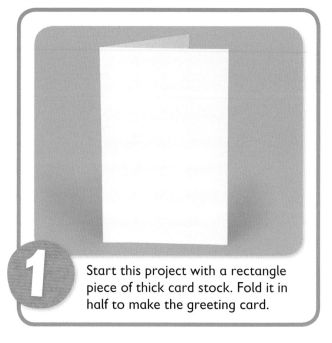

**1** Start this project with a rectangle piece of thick card stock. Fold it in half to make the greeting card.

**2** Cut colored balloon shapes from paper and glue them onto the card. Try to have them **overlapping**.

**3** Use a felt-tip pen to draw a wiggly line from each balloon. These lines are the strings tied to the balloons.

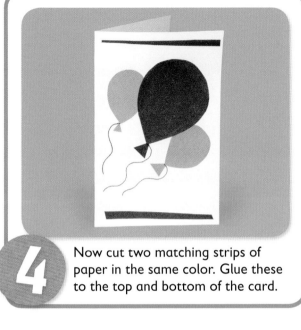

**4** Now cut two matching strips of paper in the same color. Glue these to the top and bottom of the card.

**5** Use a felt-tip pen to write a message on the front of your card. Try to do this in your best handwriting.

**6** You can make fun greeting cards for all occasions using this papercraft technique.

# Papery City

To make this picture, you will need **patterned**, colored and graph paper, glue and a felt-tip pen.

**1** Start by collecting patterned papers. This could be graph paper, wrapping paper or paper cut from magazines.

**2** Use a blue sheet of paper for the background. Glue a grey strip of paper to the bottom edge.

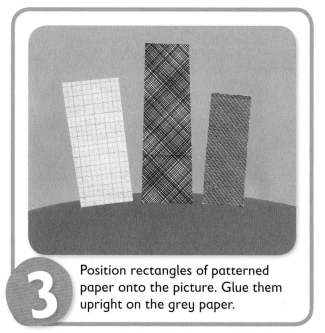

**3** Position rectangles of patterned paper onto the picture. Glue them upright on the grey paper.

**4** Glue some smaller rectangles in front of the large rectangles. You can now see the city taking shape.

**5** Glue some smaller rectangles at the very front of the picture. These are the smallest buildings.

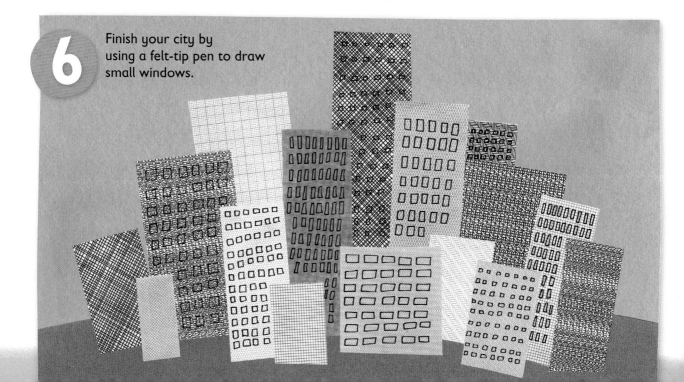

**6** Finish your city by using a felt-tip pen to draw small windows.

# Lovely Trees

This **collage** uses pictures cut from magazines. To make it, you also need colored paper and glue.

**1** Start with a large piece of pale blue paper. Glue a strip of green paper along the bottom for the grass.

**2** Cut three rectangles from a brown picture in a magazine. Glue them onto the picture for tree trunks.

**3** Use green and yellow pictures cut from magazines to create the leaves of the trees. Glue them into position.

**4** Cut grass shapes from a green magazine picture and glue these onto the green paper background.

**5** Now you can cut some circles of red paper and glue these onto each of the trees to look like apples.

**6** To finish your picture, you could glue some birds in nests onto the tree tops.

# Mighty Tractor

To make this exciting tractor scene, you will need scissors, colored paper and some glue.

**1** Start with a large piece of blue paper. Glue a strip of green paper along the bottom for the grass.

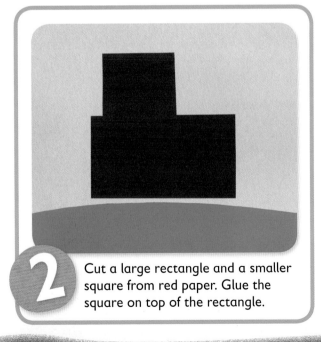

**2** Cut a large rectangle and a smaller square from red paper. Glue the square on top of the rectangle.

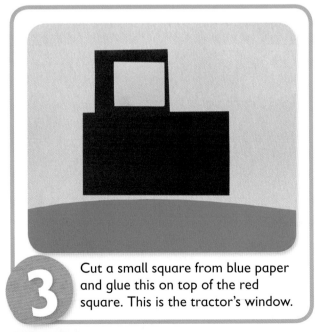

**3** Cut a small square from blue paper and glue this on top of the red square. This is the tractor's window.

**4** Glue two dark circles of different sizes onto the tractor for wheels. Add smaller, light grey circles on top.

**5** Add two strips of black paper. One is for the roof, and the other is the exhaust pipe. Glue them into place.

**6** Finish your picture by adding a little sheep, some clouds in the sky and a barn.

# Monster Mask

To make this mask, you will need a paper plate, glue, tissue paper, scissors and a felt-tip pen.

**1** Use a felt-tip pen to draw a monster's face onto a paper plate. Remember to add some big **fangs**!

**2** Rip strips of green tissue paper and glue them onto the mask. Make sure that the strips overlap each other.

**3** When the mask is covered in tissue paper, use a felt-tip pen to trace over the monster's face so it is bold.

**4** Ask an adult to cut out the eyes. Glue on white paper fangs and color in the eyebrows and nostrils.

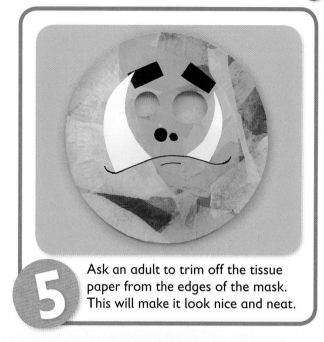

**5** Ask an adult to trim off the tissue paper from the edges of the mask. This will make it look nice and neat.

**6** Use this technique to make lots of masks. Try using other shapes and colors to create new monsters.

# Funky Cover

These colorful book covers are fun to make. You will need colored paper, scissors and glue.

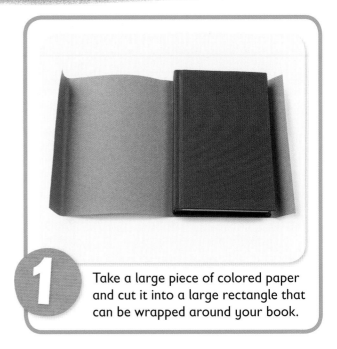

**1** Take a large piece of colored paper and cut it into a large rectangle that can be wrapped around your book.

**2** Fold the colored paper around the front of the book and tuck the edges inside the front and back cover.

**3** Now cut a rectangle from black paper. Make sure that it is slightly smaller than the front of the book.

**4** Now you can cut the black rectangle into four separate strips and glue them onto the front of the cover.

**5** The next thing to do is to decorate the four stripes. Try using colored triangles to create this zig-zag effect.

**6** Why not design some more book covers? Try gluing circles on top of each other to get a different look.

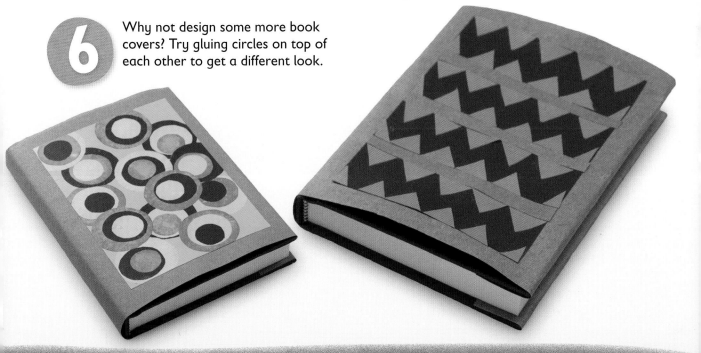

# Garden Flowers

This garden flower is easy to make. You will need a pair of scissors, glue and colored paper.

**1** Start with a large piece of pale blue paper. Glue a strip of green paper onto it for the grass.

**2** Tear strips of white paper and glue them onto the blue background. They will become clouds in the sky.

**3** Cut a thin strip of green paper to make the stem of the flower. Carefully glue this stem into place.

**4** Cut a flower shape with five round petals out of pink paper. Glue it on top of the stem.

**5** Glue a yellow paper circle onto the center of the flower. Add two green paper leaves to the base of the stem.

**6** To put finishing touches to your picture, add some other colorful flowers and a ladybug.

# Glossary

**collage** (kuh-LAHZH)  An artwork made by gluing different materials to a surface.

**fangs** (FANGZ)  Long, sharp teeth.

**materials** (muh-TEER-ee-ulz)  What things are made of.

**overlapping** (oh-ver-LAP-ing)  Resting on top of something and partly covering it.

**patterned** (PA-turnd)  Using colors and shapes that appear over and over again on something.

# Index

# Further Reading

Henry, Sandi. *Cut-Paper Play!* Dazzling Creations from Construction Paper. Portland, OR: Exodus Books, 1997.

Lewis, Amanda. *The Jumbo Book of Paper Crafts*. Toronto, ON: Kids Can Press, 2002.

# Websites

For web resources related to the subject of this book, go to: www.windmillbooks.com/weblinks and select this book's title.